THE MAGNETIC FORCE OF THE SHERO WITHIN

❧

Jyoti Khamare

ISBN: 978-1-948777-38-4

TABLE OF CONTENTS

Dedication

*I would like to dedicate this book to my loving family and
to my soul sisters around the world*

INTRODUCTION

The obstacles that women face in today's society pose challenges for us to find the space to truly give ourselves the love and attention that we need to thrive as individuals. With the emergence of the #MeToo movement and more women establishing roles in positions of power, our voices are increasingly being heard and respected. For decades, women have focused on breaking the glass ceiling and accomplishing their goals despite what society tells them they are capable of. Yet, there still remain major issues that not only silence us, but stifle our ability to put ourselves first. All women can relate to experiences where they felt unheard or objectified; the subtle sexism clouds our ambition in a traditionally male-dominated society. From the lack of power for women to vote on our reproductive rights to the pay gap, we find ourselves prone to feeling like a smaller and less significant part of the population. This can be reflected in the way we view ourselves as individuals. This book will take you through a journey of self-discovery toward self-empowerment; as you learn more about yourself, you will understand the importance of putting yourself first and you will learn how to tap into your Inner Power. This journey will bring you closer to women like yourself whether you are a business owner, a mother, or a young adult figuring out how to navigate the unknown waters.

My experiences as a woman are paramount to my mission. My past experiences shaped the way I handled my traumas and the way I envisioned my future. These unhealthy perceptions were deeply rooted in my adult experience where I find myself, even today, still learning to redefine my purpose. Before I discovered my purpose, I struggled to understand how to handle traumatic experiences (such as an abusive relationship). This resulted in me making the impulsive decision to run away from home at sixteen as a way to deal with my pain and find the answers to the endless questions I had about who I was. As I blossomed into the woman I am today, I was more equipped to handle what life threw at me. When my father passed away, and I went through sexual assault shortly after, my strength was challenged once again. However, this time around, I held on to who I am and focused on the lessons my past experiences taught me. I strongly believe that within each woman, like myself, there exists an uncovered Power that has always been there.

Life will always throw the unexpected your way and that is what makes it so important to face your self-discovery head-on. You have to let that uncertainty fuel your desire to build your strength. It is with hopes that, by taking you on my journey to how I discovered my own power, I can help you uncover yours and find hope by pushing through the darkness. Your goals are the driving force to your growth, and it all comes down to understanding the why and the how. For some women, it can be difficult to identify what their goals are in life since they might be swamped by family duties or perhaps years of not enough attention to their own self-care. It is important to reflect on your potential as an individual, irrespective of your experiences. Even after you have defined your goals, the journey still hasn't even begun. There are levels of consciousness you must pass through to get "unstuck" and evolve the hidden Power within yourself. With the right guidance and tools, your journey can feel more like a shared experience with other women that feel the way you do, and less like a lonely trek in the unknown woods. Reaching out to other women who feel as stuck as you do will not only help you, but it can also help them. Ultimately, it will help you both in creating the most powerful tool of sisterhood.

CHAPTER 1

THE BIRTH OF YOUR

EMPOWERMENT

~

H er eyes, as they bored deeply into mine, were brimmed with unshakeable strength and gentle compassion. Her face glowed with the spirit of a woman so in love with who she was, despite what she had gone through. She was a deeply grounded oak tree with a sturdy trunk that was once a fragile sapling emerging from a young acorn in the soil. The endurance she encompassed was prevalent in the way she held herself as she looked back at me reassuringly. I smiled to myself, watching my eyes light up as my reflection smiled back at me.

We all come from a seed of some sort. One of the most beautiful things about trees is that no matter where their roots are placed, their magnificence is always a result of their environment. With that being said, I strongly believe that no matter what you have been through, you are the only one in control of how you water your roots to reach the heights you deserve. Like a resilient tree in the woods, you must grow toward the sunlight at every opportunity you get and in spite of every obstacle in your way. Tap into your inner power to understand what treatment your personal growth requires because, although I could give you all the tools and experiences that worked for me, it would only serve as a guide for what would work for you.

One of the most profound experiences that shaped me into the powerful woman I am today stemmed from growing up in the complex American society as a Desi girl. Many Indian women can identify with coming back home after an eventful day in high school to the aromatic smell of Biryani and the loving chatter of their mother in the kitchen. At times, I felt like an utterly different person at home than at school. At school, I was the girl catching up on the recent gossip by the lockers.

Walking through our front door was like a subconscious switch in the way I walked, spoke, and carried myself. As a young girl, the culture clash was often difficult to navigate, especially with everything the typical American teenage girl had on her plate. The dynamics this experience brought with it added to the extra frustration that, at the time, I was not sure how to navigate. For as long as I could remember, I would wake up to the sound of my mom listening to her bhajans. As with many Indian families, we celebrated marriages, engagements, Diwali, and other festivals with joy in our hearts. We celebrated when we were able to. We'd dress up, eat all sorts of scrumptious Indian desserts, and

dance the night away with other Hindu families in the community — some celebrations even last a couple of weekends. My parents frequently chided me for not knowing our religious scriptures by heart, with our prayers taking place mostly on the weekends and when we attended temple. These were all the little things that shaped the woman I grew up to become. Even today, I still find myself instinctively taking off my shoes before entering
a home.

Although I can easily identify with the American teenage experience, my childhood and adolescent years were just so different from my peers. Watching American movies and reading books on the woeful teenage drama of prom dates and high school hierarchies helped me better understand how to blend in. However, the more I tried to step into that identity, the more disconnected I felt from who I truly was. It was deeper than just fitting in. I felt so confused and lost about my identity. It was painfully obvious that there were no brown women in a majority of the movies I watched. Those that did have some sort of representation either completely misrepresented my culture or had the Indian girl as the sidekick to the main character. It was difficult to find the pride in my culture that I have today, and consequently, a challenge to accept myself. To make matters even more of a challenge, there were times when I would get teased about the color of my skin. However, there was always a presence that stood much taller than any situation ever could.

BULLIED by the kids in school about the things they just didn't understand. It ranged from the color of my skin, to the kids asking me why Indian people dress so different?. to the curry-filled aroma that my friends noticed when entering my home. American kids can just be so insensitive, which meant that instead of inquiring to learn more, they resorted to teasing and laughing. As a young girl, this made me feel so different from the kids around me, so it was easy to point a finger of blame at my Indian ethnicity. One of the earliest experiences that stood out to me was when I was around six or seven years of age, and I was the only kid that was put on the honor roll. My parents placed a huge emphasis on education — which was expected given that it was education that gave them the American dream opportunity — so I started off school carefully groomed to strive for the best. However, when I showed up to get my award, I was shocked to see that I was the only one who got put on the honor roll. It threw me off, especially since the other kids got upset, and it made me feel isolated from the rest of my peers at a really young age. This experience was really important to me because I felt, for the first time, that I shouldn't be smart. I suddenly felt reserved and began the process of building up a wall to protect myself, and this took many years into adulthood to unlearn.

What was even more confusing than the sharp contrast between who I was at home and the person I was around my American friends was the Indian community's expectations of my future. In the traditional Indian culture, it was expected that I would graduate with high honors, pursue higher education, and get married to a parent-approved Indian man. While my American friends' parents sighed with defeat at their defiant teenagers that were sent into a frenzy at the idea of chores, I gave in and did what I had to do around the house to reassure my parents that I too, would make a great Indian wife. As we neared graduation, my American friends relished at the thought of finally moving out, while I held back my shock at the possibility that there were parents who gave their kids this much freedom in the choices for their future. Burdened by all these expectations and duties, I couldn't find the right way to communicate how I felt about the future my parents envisioned for me. How could I bring myself to not only disappoint them but shed light on how I really felt about their life decisions?

My parents were both born and raised in India. They moved to the United States for better opportunities and to grow their careers. My mother grew up on a farm near the Himalayas. Her life was one of fun. She would run around and joyfully help the farm workers — if she wanted to —, learn Indian Bhajans in the evening with her sisters, and attend school during the day. She would spend her day at school receiving high grades then, in the evenings, she would help her mom prepare dinner and say her prayers. My mother obtained a college-level education before getting married, and she worked hard to become a nurse after being married and having children. It was this disciplined lifestyle that defined her work ethic, and I found it so admirable. It was also the commitment that was needed to be able to build the life she built in America.

My parents' marriage, like many in the Indian culture, was an arranged one. My father was a veterinarian in America, so her parents approved of the marriage and encouraged their daughter to get to know him better in preparation for tying the knot.

My relationship with my parents was a loving one, but there was definitely no shortage of misunderstandings and frustration from both ends. My father was very strict, but he also made sure to spend time with my brother and me to build the father-child bond that he valued above all else. We would always grab breakfast together, and he would give us his morning lectures on the kind of individuals he envisioned us growing up to be. It took me a while to see that their overprotective nature was just a reflection of their deep love for us, and not something that they realized was limiting to my self-discovery. Since they didn't grow up in America like I did, it was understandable that their wishes for my future (including an arranged marriage) were coming from a good place.

By going on this journey together, and with the help of the tools that I will share with you in the process, we can find the key to open your hidden doors and bring light to your inner power. The first step is to tap into your past experiences and reflect on what direction you see yourself going. By the end of this journey, you should have started to build a relationship both with yourself and with the Higher Power. This is critical to do before you can expect to start to see the results reflected in different parts of your life. When I think of this stage, I imagine a caterpillar in its cocoon. Before it can grow its beautiful, large wings that will help it fly over any obstacle in its way, it must spend some time alone developing its wings. By spending this time in your cocoon, focused on developing this internal relationship, you will find yourself naturally deflecting this positive energy into all aspects of your life. Your relationships with others will also reflect the internal strength of the relationship that you have with yourself. Your inner power will manifest in the way your mindset develops, helping you tap into your super consciousness. From there, it may seem almost effortless, but it is truly a result of the subtle build-up of small victories in the journey of growth. You will begin to see changes in your business, finances, and success as a woman. It all begins and is a result of becoming one with your inner power.

CHAPTER 2

THE PROCESS

~

When we hear the word "intelligence," our mind may jump to high test scores, academic achievements, mathematical abilities, or the contributions to scientific research. However, little do we know, this form of intelligence is just one of the three types of intelligence. While our material accomplishments and advancements in our career often require us to build this type of intelligence, without the other pillars of intellectual development, we will have difficulty propelling ourselves forward to accomplishing our goals. The first type of intelligence, which I have already touched on briefly, is Rational Intelligence. The popular Intelligence Quotient (IQ) is measured through tests, along with other numerical measures of intelligence found in our education systems. Rational intelligence refers to our logical, rule-bound and problem-solving intelligence. It is a style of thinking that can be trained through repetitive applied practice of skills. This intelligence is important because it is what helps us function so we are capable of completing day-to-day tasks. The second type of intelligence, the Emotional Quotient (EQ), refers to our Emotional Intelligence. To put this simply, this form of intelligence is what our hearts and emotions have. It is manifested through our trust, empathy, emotional self-awareness, and self-control. Emotional Intelligence is so important when it comes to building and maintaining relationships, be it your partner or a stranger. If you were to walk into a store to complain about their services and found the shop owner looking upset, someone in tune with their emotional intelligence would take this as a sign that perhaps now isn't the best time to give the store owner negative feedback. The third and final type of intelligence is Spiritual Intelligence, which is a foundational core of rational and emotional intelligence. The Spiritual Quotient (SQ) is measured by the ability to access higher meanings, values, abiding purposes, and unconscious aspects of the self. An individual with spiritual intelligence is one who is able to leverage these qualities to find a purpose in living and create a richer and more creative life.

Let's go back to the analogy of an oak tree in the context of intellect. The root of the oak tree symbolizes your spiritual intelligence. It holds the tree firm in the ground and provides the nourishment to keep it alive. The trunk, extending so elegantly and twisting itself around obstacles to push the leaves to sunlight, is symbolic of your emotional intelligence. The branches, extending over nearby trees and spreading open to the outside world, represent your rational intelligence. Together, these provide you, the tree, stability to withstand the changing environment around you and reach unimaginable heights. Once the majestic oak tree has peaked past the darkness of the woods, it can now grow bountiful leaves to absorb the light it worked so hard to reach. These leaves, your healthy habits, are paramount in ensuring that you reap the benefits of your inevitable growth and resilience by growing beautiful flowers. These flowers are representative of your successes, from career success to your relationship with your body to your financial prosperity. You are now a flourishing tree, with not just the physical, emotional, and spiritual strength, but you also have the visible results to keep you striving toward even bigger goals. Once your flowers have bloomed, you are now able to drop acorns nearby and leave your mark and impact on Earth. You can now help others grow and inspire their own journey to reaching heights like yours. From a distance, the awe-inspiring magnificence of a wise old oak tree that has stood the test of time and weather conditions may appear to be for the very obvious reason that the oak tree is simply built to be strong. However, speak to any botanist, and they will inform you, quite plainly, that if an oak tree was to be in a toxic environment (of chemical herbicides for example), then the tree will fail to blossom for very long. Similarly, if the oak tree's roots came into contact with another tree's roots that were infected with tree rot, then in time, the oak tree will fail to stand up as strongly and will eventually crash to the ground in defeat.

So how does this apply to our own health? The way I see it is that if you allow external negativity, be it from your loved ones or society, to enter your surrounding environment, you are bound to be affected by it. It is so much easier said than done to not allow yourself to be impacted by your surroundings. However, there are stages in your life where you are most vulnerable to this negativity. For this reason, you must either remove yourself from these toxins, or remove them from your life by setting healthy boundaries. Most of the population is functioning from an unconscious level and from being conditioned by their roles. People can unknowingly hurt your emotional growth, sway your spiritual grounding, and affect the development of your intellectual understanding. The way I ensured that I was focused during my own journey was to make sure that the life I was living was the life I knew would make me happy. That is key to watering your roots and ensuring that your growth is a healthy one. It may sound oversimplified to say that the primary nourishment for your growth is knowing what you want in order to be happy but that is really what it comes down to. For this reason, I had to sit down and really reflect and be real with myself. I had to put aside society's expectations of who I should become and how to become it. This process requires that you get to know yourself for who you really are. What might help my tree grow may not be what your tree needs in order to grow. Often, people confuse the process by searching for their flowers while they are still little saplings. They fail to understand that the flowers are a result of the growth, and they will not appear right away. We should keep an inner knowing that everything works out in Divine timing and we will start to see evidence. When you define your progress by visible success, you are very likely to be frustrated. Instead, we should see our progress as growth and realize it is not a race, it is an adventure. With that being said, it is so important for us to focus on ourselves so that we can allow the natural attraction to lead us to our dream job position, materialistic aspirations, and even our complementary partner who will help us reach our heights. Another mistake we tend to make as a society is putting deadlines on our growth process based on time, not on experience. We are all humans who are on different

paths to the same destination of sunlight, or in other words happiness, peace, and interconnectivity with those around us.

So now that we understand the importance of spiritual, emotional, and rational intelligence as a foundation for prospering in all aspects of our life, we can use these three intelligences to some degree since each of them supports our survival in a different way. Some of us may be strong in one and weak in the others? however, we are able to nurture them as we grow to develop our foundation. I will be guiding you through this process, every step of the way, with what I found worked best for me. You are in no obligation to limit yourself to proceed through this path in the exact same way and order that I did. To make this guide as effective as possible, I suggest that you simply experience each step with me. We will go through it together as you apply the lessons, I have to share with you. Please take notes whenever you resonate with something. From there, you can start to take the steps to change your life.

The first aspect of the dynamic journey of self-discovery and manifestation of our goals is spiritual empowerment. By planting my roots of spirituality, I was able to truly explore who I was as an entity separate from my surrounding environment and physical ambitions. The first signs that you should look for when becoming one with the power within yourself is developing the ability to think outside the box; it is a sense of humility to access energies that come from something beyond the ego, yourself, and your day-to-day concerns. We all, at some point, reach a point in our lives where we get in touch with that higher self. No matter what your religious beliefs are, or even if you don't have any, this sense of interconnectivity with an internal power is an experience we can all relate to. In fact, research shows that around seventy percent of adults around the world, irrespective of their culture, education, or background, have had some sort of "peak experiences." These peak experiences may not be phrased as "getting in touch with an inner power," but they are nevertheless significant internal realizations that helped shape or change their path in life. If you are not sure if you have experienced what we call these "peak experiences," then you need to step back and begin the reflection process. Ask yourself, when was the last time you felt that suddenly everything was beautiful, there was a sense of oneness to being, and that love permeates the world?. This feeling is felt by your entire being; it often flashes by very quickly and is gone faster than it came. These moments usually come after some sort of healing process from an experience where you finally feel like you have stepped outside a tunnel that seemed to be endless. It can also feel like you've finally received what you have been working so long for, yet we're so close to giving up on. On an even deeper level, they might even come when you take a seat outside alone and really listen to the world around you, paying no attention to the chatter in your mind. If this is not something you have felt yet, that is okay too. This experience tends to shake people and not many people feel like opening up about them. Together, we will go through the process of getting more in touch with your inner power through spirituality so that you can begin manifesting this profound sense of self-empowerment into all aspects of your life.

The second aspect of the journey is found within our mind. Unlike our spiritual intelligence, this part heavily relies on our behavioral patterns that are based on our emotional and rational intelligence. Although our spiritual intelligence will help greatly in the way we see ourselves and thus how we speak to ourselves, it comes down to the habits we allow ourselves to have on a daily basis. When we look at the connection between body, mind, and spirit, what we are really talking about is the energy of our feelings and emotions, which are the languages of the spirit. The mind governs our mental and emotional aspects. It is where we find consciousness, which drives our awareness of the world around us, and is the power behind our ability to think. Our consciousness is housed within our minds, and it is made up of our Superconscious, Subconscious, and Conscious psyches. Our mind is also made up of our emotions, which consists of our feelings. Our feelings cannot be seen. They can only be felt. Each emotion is unique and is expressed differently for every person. For this reason alone, it is important to be in tune with how you express yourself — figure out what triggers each emotion and how to navigate through each one. It is through our mind, and thus emotions, that we are able to find who we are. This is how we are able to determine what our likes and dislikes are. We tap into our inner wants and desires so that we can strive toward what we want to accomplish. The most important thing when it comes to our mind is to acknowledge and validate our emotions no matter where they are on the spectrum of negative to positive. We all have bad days, weeks, months, or even years. This can make it difficult to see the positive in things, and our minds tend to focus on everything that may be going wrong. It should therefore be a commitment to yourself and your mind to reground yourself through Words of Affirmation as a means to truly listen to the language your spirit chooses to express itself through. Be gentle with yourself and let yourself feel what it needs to achieve balance. Maybe this means taking a long drive, walking in the park, or even fully immersing yourself in a self-care day. As you start to tend to yourself and go inward, you may begin to feel drawn to certain things and ideas will start to reveal themselves. It is then that you will start to change your perspective on views you may have held on tightly to.

The third aspect of the journey is the relationship between you and your body. When we explore the connection between body, mind, and spirit, we discover how connected or disconnected our body is from our mind and emotions. When we take a look around us, one of the things that we all have in common is that we each have a body that houses our mind and spirit. This body is the vessel that holds our brain and body parts, and it is made up of trillions of cells. These cells build our tissues, nerves, bones, and organs into the physical body that we recognize as ourselves. When we think about our relationship with our body, we must connect with every aspect that holds us together physically and mentally. When our mind is not at peace, we can feel our heart rate increase, our head throb, our palms get sweaty, and our focus diminishing. When we experience disease or pain, our entire being is affected and it is so much more difficult to complete day-to-day tasks. To be in tune with how our body communicates with us through symptoms and physical sensations is more than just respecting our internal mind and ensuring that we are giving our spirit the chance to be heard, really listened to, and cared for. By allowing our body to communicate with us, we can set boundaries for ourselves and make sure that we are always as healthy as we can possibly be.

Ultimately, our body, mind, and spirit are intimately connected and rely on each other. When integrated, they complete our human essence and allow us to move forward from a place of wholeness. Because these three parts of our being are so interconnected, our process must involve all three. Without this, we will always feel like something is missing. These might feel overwhelming to approach, as they are very complex aspects of our progress to self-empowerment. For this reason, I always suggest we break it down to the basics. A good place to start is to build a healthy and organized routine. This routine should include something from each of the three aspects of your journey. Every single day, you must do something that nourishes your body, feeds your mind, and grounds your spirit. This requires that you make time for yourself every day, no matter what is going on around you. To do this, you must learn how to identify unhealthy habits, distinguish what makes a healthy relationship with those around you, and most importantly, set boundaries with everything in your life. You must be able to draw the line at relationships with friends and family that don't help you serve your inner purpose.

These boundaries you set for yourself will not only give you the freedom to work on these three aspects of your self-empowerment, but they will also allow you the space to build a positive relationship with your finances too. Financial empowerment is not often talked about when we address self-discovery. It is undeniable that money gives you the ability to treat yourself and gives you the materialistic freedom to go for the life you deserve. It is only fair then that you acknowledge the importance of financial empowerment. Through these various healthy habits that you build, you will uncover your inner power, tap into your superconscious, and accomplish the goals you set out to achieve. Money is a resource that was made from nature to support us on our journey and to enrich our life and the lives of others. Money can be created through your own unique way in which you would like to achieve change in the world for the greater good of all. The more you establish a relationship with money, you will understand it is there to support you and it is your birthright. Money is not bad; it is needed for all and it is waiting for you to receive it. We have been conditioned to view money as hard to get, hard work, and maybe even evil. The inner dialogue you have toward money affects your relationship with it. In spirituality, you see how we are deeply connected to everything around us and to nature, the mother. If you were to look up what money is made of, you will notice that it is that very nature that this resource is made from.

CHAPTER 3

SPIRITUAL EMPOWERMENT

~

Like emotions, our spirit is invisible to us and to others. Unlike our mind and body however, our spirit is innately healthy and cannot be in an unhealthy state. It is for this reason that we must make the time every day to find a way to connect with the Higher Power found within us. Our spirit is a direct expression of life's creator. Depending on your religious beliefs, this might be Divinity, Source, God, or The Universe. Through your spirit, you can find what your individual creative expressions are. More importantly, your spirit can connect you to something that is much bigger than yourself and your five senses. The most beautiful thing about this is that the spirit will always be whole, untouched, and in a positive state. Whatever we go through mentally or physically, our spirit remains unaffected. It simply witnesses and guides us through life and allows us to truly experience who we are. By becoming one with your spirit, you are taking the first step to self-empowerment.

The word "spirituality" is derived from the Latin word spiritus, which denotes soul, courage, vigor, and breath[1]. Within the word itself is the Power that can be uncovered by synchronizing with our inner spirituality. Through this revelation, you are able to find the strength to accomplish your goals. Spirit is quite literally, like the oxygen we breathe; it is necessary for our being. To understand the importance of spirituality, we must understand the impact of its absence. Without the roots of spirituality, a tree will cease to grow and flourish. The roots do more than just anchor and support the heavy tree. They reach deep into the ground to absorb the water we provide it and the minerals we feed it. When these are not readily available, the tree roots burrow deeper into the ground and spread far across its physical location to reach the nourishment it needs. When these roots find what is needed to not just survive, but blossom to their full capacity, it absorbs the nutrients and water to hold it in for when the tree needs it most. In winter, or when times get hard, the stored nutrients and water provide the tree the strength it needs to function and focus on reaching the heights it strives for. These roots of spirituality are fundamental to keeping you on the right track, no matter what you are experiencing. When we disconnect from our spirituality, we lose the grounding and nourishment needed to build and maintain our

---

[1] Oxford Languages

emotional and rational Intelligence and be in tune with our physical body.

The process of spiritual empowerment is necessary as a means to gain clarity. There are many ways one can become one with their inner power through spirituality. It all begins with setting the time aside to connect with God. The process may differ for each individual, depending on their spiritual beliefs and what makes them comfortable, but I always suggest starting off by creating an environment where you can be yourself. Make a space at home where you can be truly alone with your body and mind in one place. There must be no distractions or noise that will dampen the connection between you and your inner power. If there are distractions or maybe you desire more silence, pick up a pair of headphones or put-up heavy curtains to help achieve a more tranquil atmosphere. This might even be sitting outside near nature, which is the closest thing to a spiritual connection with our environment. I also always suggest to light your favorite candle since it will help create a sense of comfort associated with your spiritual connection each time you come back to it. Be aware of what works best for you and how you best communicate with yourself and others, then apply that awareness to your spiritual connection. Those who express themselves best through writing can journal this experience, while those who prefer verbal communication may speak to themselves. You can try to place your hand over your heart and just speak of what you are wanting and let your communication be open and more heard. Try to do this daily. For the religious, a prayer might be the best way to connect with your inner power and talking to God will be key for your spiritual empowerment. However, this must not be left at your meditation, as you must remain in touch with your spirituality throughout the day. See your inner power as your most valued friend, and ask for guidance throughout the day. By doing this, you are strengthening your relationship with your inner power while maintaining the manifestation of the relationship into your day-to-day life. As you start to enhance your openness to the spiritual world, you should simply ask for protection for your greater good.

Much like a dancer perfecting her pirouette, which is considered one of the most difficult of ballet dance moves, the process of achieving spiritual empowerment takes multiple attempts and repetitions before you will begin to feel the progress. The most important thing is that you do not beat yourself up if you forget or life gets busy, just do what feels right for you. To some, this might be felt in their first meditation. For others, it may take weeks or even months to begin to feel the difference. You can try different approaches and find one that you resonate with the most; we all are unique, and that is the beauty of it. Trusting and surrendering to the process, both the easy and the difficult, will be the driving force of getting you to that peak of empowerment and uncovering your Hidden Power within you. I always encourage that you read on others' experiences with spirituality, and use the path that makes the most sense to you as an individual. Danah Zohar, an American-

British author and speaker on physics and philosophy, coined the term "spiritual intelligence." She defined twelve principles underlying spiritual intelligence[2]. When we look at the physical world in biology, complex adaptive systems are living systems that create order out of chaos. Because these systems are highly unstable, it also makes them hypersensitive, allowing them to be holistic in their response to their ever-changing environment. Similarly, our spirit is constantly in a creative dialogue with our surrounding environment. Within each one of us, we find a consciously adaptive system that interacts with our environment physically and mentally. Therefore, by going through these twelve principles that our spiritual intelligence is built on, I am also touching on its connection to our physical and mental being.

The first principle of spiritual intelligence is Self-Awareness. This is the knowledge of what you believe in and value, and what deeply motivates you. This must not be confused with emotional self-awareness, which is the ability to know what we are feeling at any given moment. spiritual self-awareness involves you really getting to know who you are. It means to recognize what you care for, what you live for, and what you would be willing to forgive, even if it may be challenging. To have spiritual self-awareness, you must be willing to live true to yourself while respecting others. This authenticity

---

[2] Spiritual Intelligence : The Ultimate Intelligence

manifests in the genuineness of your communication with your deeper self, which then allows you to bring yourself into the outer world through actions. In order to develop Self-Awareness, you must be able to ask yourself the right questions. Do you have a sense of what your long-term goals and strategies are? Close your eyes and picture yourself thirty years from now and really let your imagination have an unlimited, measureless lift-off. Think about the clothes you're wearing, the people you're talking to, and the feelings you are experiencing — really tap into your senses in that moment before bringing yourself back to the present. Write down what you experienced to help you find the answer to this question. From there, you can bring yourself to the next question. How do you anticipate the impact of your actions on those around you? Practice this in your day-to-day conversations with your loved ones and with strangers. Communication with others and actions you take must always have some intention behind it and being self-aware means you are sensitive to how they impact others. Finally, take a look at your personal strengths and weaknesses and their connection to how the outside world sees them. We all have strengths and weaknesses and they are not there to by any means dishearten you. They are there so we can focus on our strengths and move toward what we want to create. This takes being honest with yourself and having conversations with others to help you gain perspective through trusted self-discernment.

The second principle of spiritual intelligence is spontaneity, which is being able to live in and be responsive to the moment. Often mistaken for acting impulsively, it is actually behavior that is manifested by self-discipline, practice, and self-control; it is built on responsibility. When you think back to your childhood traumas, prejudices from society, assumptions, values, and projections, Spontaneity allows you to let go of these barriers holding you back and be more aware of the moment. A spontaneous act could be something as simple as buying a plant to commit to care for, or something as challenging as taking up violin lessons. To be spontaneous means you are prepared to experiment and take the risks needed to grow, just as you are doing now by picking up this book to challenge yourself. You are prepared to follow your instincts to work toward what will add value to your life and seek opportunities to enjoy the process of growth.

The third principle is Being Vision and Value-Led. To do this, your actions must be aligned with your principles and deep beliefs. The first time I became aware of my inner purpose was when I had just come out of an abusive relationship. The traumatic experience led me on a spiral of self-reflection where I began to question my place in the world. I was quite young and it took a few years to get clear on what I wanted to achieve in life. I had just run away from home and was thrown into a world of reality that I was far from prepared to deal with. By the time I was back home, I was determined to live a life that was for the betterment of those around me. I was still lost in life though, and I did get through an experimental stage. I remained rebellious, but I was more aware of my right to have whatever it was that I wanted. I wanted to leave the world a better place than I found it and make a difference with my actions. Coming back home and having a conversation with my father made me realize that what I create out of my life must always be aligned with what my heart desires. After finishing nursing school after a few years had passed, I did notice the signs. Signs that you are abiding by your deep beliefs are speaking out when you feel like your workplace is failing to live by its stated values, making career decisions by a desire to do something that is worthwhile, and finding yourself ready to fight for what matters to you.

The next principle of Spiritual Intelligence is Holism, which brings everything into perspective through your ability to see patterns and connections. Holism is what gives you the sense of belonging. When we take a look at the physical world, Holism can be found in the way that systems become so integrated that each part is defined by every other part of the system. When you woke up this morning and made your cup of coffee, the smell that drifted through your kitchen may have been carried to your next-door neighbor. This simple shared experience creates a moment where two individuals feel something as a result of something as simple as a scent. What you think, feel, and value affects the whole world around you. By living a Holistic life, you are taking on the responsibility to be a cooperative part of the community. Lack of Holism gives birth to competition and separates us from each other. Holism can also be reflected in your deeper understanding of how everything operates, the anticipation of long-term consequences of today's decisions, and strengthens your balance between a working and non-working life.

Compassion is the fifth principle and is defined as having the quality of deep empathy. To be compassionate means that not only do you acknowledge others' feelings, but you also feel them on a personal level. When I experienced sexual assault, I am grateful that I had embodied Compassion after years of self-reflection and activating my spiritual activities. While I fully accept that I had to recover, I never went to a counselor. I actually healed through my spirituality and that was my own healing that occurred. I was more capable of seeing it from the perpetrator's perspective. They were acting out a place of pain and from there, and I was able to take back the Power and overcome the pain I felt. I was able to release it with divine love and acceptance. With Compassion, I was able to understand the enemy and transcend the trauma.

The sixth principle is Celebration of Diversity, which is very closely related to Compassion. When we think of diversity, we might think back to our past diversity training at work or our experiences as minorities in a predominantly White-American society. However, what this means is diversity of thought. Looking back at my childhood growing up as an Indian in America, there was a deeper level of diversity of thought within my surroundings, both at home and in school. One of the biggest struggles I had was finding who I was in the midst of the completely different perspectives my parents had compared to my friends at school. One one hand, I loved my parents yet disagreed with their opinions. On the other hand, I supported many of the American values such as the freedom to choose who you want to love and marry, but simply did not feel like I belonged. The confusion consumed me until I learnt the Power of Celebration of Diversity. By accepting my parents' opinion and owning my own perspective as valid, I was able to find peace within myself. A person who has mastered their Celebration of Diversity makes sure to take into consideration various perspectives when planning, respects ideas that are not aligned with their perspective, and encourages individuality. Make sure to not only be this person, but surround yourself with these kinds of people so that you are not limiting your full potential.

The next principles of spiritual intelligence are the complementary pair of Field Independence and Humility. Field Independence, derived from psychology, is representative of the strength that comes from being able to stand up for what you believe, even if it isn't the popular opinion. On the flip side, Humility is the recognition that your opinion may be wrong and therefore requires that you are constantly checking yourself to make sure that your perspective is validated by others' experiences. Finding the right balance between the two is pivotal for how you make use of your spiritual intelligence for the betterment of your growth and for society. When I ran away from home at sixteen, I felt like a bird in a cage that had finally found its way out and had flown for the very first time. It was the first time in my life that I truly felt like I was finally practicing Field Independence, even though I was definitely falling short on the other principles of spiritual intelligence. After returning to the loving arms of my family shortly after the eye-opening experience, I learnt the Power of Humility. The experience was one of the peak points of my enlightenment because I was able to hit two birds with one stone in the process of trying to fly out of my own cage. Little did I know, had I embodied Celebration of Diversity, all I needed to do was communicate with my parents so that they could understand my pain.

As you near the peak of your spiritual journey, you will find yourself asking the right questions. The final principles of spiritual intelligence include the tendency to ask the why questions, the ability to reframe yourself and turn negative life events into positive learning experiences, and the development of an innate sense that you are being called upon to serve and give something back to others. The reason why we must go through the previous steps before reaching this stage is comfort. Asking ourselves the right questions can be frightening, especially because there aren't easy answers to these questions. For as long as I can remember, I have wanted to be a nurse just like my mum. Of course, like many of us do, I drifted away from this goal as I went through different stages in my life. Holding back from giving my all to my studies in fear of bringing unwanted attention to my academic success in high school was one of the reasons why I wasn't sure if I was the right fit for such a demanding career. When I reached this point of my spirituality, I began to ask the why questions that really challenged my self-image. Why do I want to be a nurse? Why do I not feel like I am the right fit to work toward something I've always dreamed of becoming? Why can't I find confidence in my rational intelligence? From there, I was able to step back and reframe to look at the bigger picture. I was more clearheaded about what my goals were and my mind completely shifted to looking at the long-term objectives. I was now able to truly recognize, accept, and own my mistake of giving in to what others thought about me. This Positive Use of Adversity allowed me to forgive myself for being the one holding myself back, and I found that I no longer blamed my experience as a kid for being the only one on the honor roll. It takes so much courage to face our adversities with acknowledgement of the role we played in limiting ourselves because of past mistakes. Suddenly, I felt the reserved energy completely flow out of me. The simple words, "I made a mistake, and I am now going to move forward in a different direction" can do wonders in changing your entire mindset. By practicing Positive Use of Adversity, we are able to recognize that we will inevitably go through hardships in our lives. It is part of the human experience. These experiences empower us when spirituality allows us to open up our minds to our full potential by not allowing our mistakes to limit who we aspire to become. At this point, you will be more in touch with the inner power and might find yourself exploring the principle of Sense of Vocation, where you feel like you have a calling from the Higher Power to help others build a strong relationship with their own spirituality. The Sense of Vocation may manifest as an overwhelming desire to give back. This principle sums up spiritual intelligence as you reach ultimate alignment.

By now, you should be getting a much better understanding of the interconnectedness of the different principles of spiritual intelligence. Your experiences in life will guide you through the necessary lessons needed to align with all the different aspects of spirituality. For many of us, this may take us almost our entire life. For some, we might find this alignment earlier on. No matter how long it takes you, know that it is completely acceptable and should be embraced. I found that when I became more aligned with my spirituality, I was able to reinvent myself and overcome challenges with peace and self-love. By learning more about these different principles and opening your mind to the world of spirituality, you are taking the first step to uncovering your inner power through the first principle of self-awareness. With that being said, you have just initiated the journey to uncover your inner power through spiritual empowerment.

CHAPTER 4

WORDS OF AFFIRMATION

~

As you climb the ladder of spiritual empowerment, you will begin to notice whenever you drift off from your central grounding. The sense of peace you get from surrendering to the process may be replaced with feelings of anxiety and constant anticipation for what is coming next. You might find your humility challenged by your ego when you get in an argument with someone you care for and find yourself becoming, once again, consumed with anger. Perhaps, instead of being able to look at the bigger picture when you get fired from your job, you find yourself spiraling into a state of depression. Through our emotions and mental health patterns, we are able to understand when our spirit is communicating with us. Those who may not be in touch with their spirituality may feel overwhelmed by this storm of emotions. They may feel that they are to blame for the external circumstances and fail to apply the various principles of spiritual intelligence to manifest their inner power as a way to overcome these obstacles. For this reason, I always encourage the use of words of affirmation. When you hear that term, you might think of the love language that we use for our partners. While this is also important, what I mean here is the love language you reserve for yourself — to remind your mind who you are, what you deserve, and what your potential is. It is even more important to constantly remind yourself than it is to reach this stage of self-empowerment because if we do not maintain practice and keep our mind at this stage, our progress will cease to be as effective.

Whenever I have a friend, family, or stranger ask me for advice on how they should remain self-empowered I tell them, "You are the CEO of your own life." What I mean by this is that everyone is completely in charge of the direction their life goes, even if things do not go as planned. When we take a look at the duties and responsibilities of a CEO, it can help make this analogy much clearer. A CEO, which is the highest-ranking executive in a company, is responsible for making all the decisions, managing the operations and resources of the company, and acting as a main point of communication. If we look at our lives as one big functioning company, then by being the CEO, you are not just floating through life. You are in charge and responsible for what happens underneath the surface. The CEO is not the person who can control what happens to the company, but rather the success and stability of the company relies on the way in which the CEO reacts to these external events. Similarly, you must not define your success by what happens around you but instead by the reaction you have to what life throws in your direction. Become one with your mind as a means of understanding what your spirit is trying to communicate with you. Make your decisions with all the spiritual principles we outlined earlier in mind and practice this daily so that you are prepared when things go wrong. All of this might appear a lot easier than it actually is, especially when things happen that really devastated and traumatize us. For this reason, similar to a CEO, we must have our resources and tools ready at all times in preparation for such an emergency that will require us to protect ourselves and our progress. This is where words of affirmation come in.

My mother always used to tell me, "An empty mind is the devil's workshop." She was always insistent on me spending more time working on myself by working hard at school, praying every day, and eating healthy. At the time, like many kids, I would get really frustrated at her for constantly reminding me not to waste time and focus on what I have to get done. Little did I know, in her own way, she was trying to help me get into the habit of working on all aspects of my Higher Intelligence by taking actions on my spirituality, body, and mind everyday. As we get older, we no longer have our parents reminding us to take care of ourselves, so we must take on the responsibility to do this for ourselves. Words of affirmation can help put the needle back to the center, helping you feel more solid and focused on staying on this path. More than keeping you on the right track, it also helps build a sense of intention. I always say that everything we do in our lives should be done with intention —from what we decide to put into our bodies to how we spend our productive time to how we choose to relax our minds. Even something as simple as taking a nap or partaking in whatever activity you deem pleasurable should be done with the intention of furthering your sense of inner peace and helping yourself be the best person you can be.

In the physical world, there is only one Force that is uniting us. Depending on your beliefs, this might be God or the Universe. By living your life with the highest intentions, you are allowing this Force to flow through you so that you can reach your full potential. Words of affirmation bring us to that force by connecting our mind and emotions to our spiritual being. There are a few words of affirmation that I find really powerful and personally use every day. The first is Thomas Troward's famous saying, "My mind is a center of Divine operation." Troward was an author that was deeply inspired by mental sciences. To truly feel the strength of this statement, we must unpack it to understand what he meant. It is important to note that he doesn't say the mind is the center of Divine operation, which means something completely different. He stresses that the mind is a center of Divine operation. In other words, all our minds are a center, not just yours or mine. This might sound confusing because when we think of an empty room, there is only one center. This applies to everything physical that is limited by boundaries of some sort. However, the Divine Higher Power is Infinite and has no boundaries. Therefore, there is not one single center but Infinite centers, which is found in each and every one of our minds. This reminds me that we are all part of the Divine. Together, we collectively make up the universal consciousness and mind and are a unified part of the Infinite. When I am reminded of this, I no longer feel alone or isolated from everything around me. Instead, my problems feel so much more digestible with the bigger picture in mind. This phrase, as simple as it may sound, brings back the connection between my mind and spirit.

Another phrase that I say to myself everyday is "I am an unlimited spiritual being." In addition to reminding myself that I am a spirit housed in a body and connected to the outside world through my mind, I am also reminding myself that I have no limits. Whatever I set my mind to accomplish can be achieved if I commit to it. I am able to speak it into existence by giving it my full attention and effort every single day. This one is one of my favorite things to say to myself because it can be so easy to limit ourselves when we get into routine habits. As a nurse, I have to stick to a very controlled work schedule and in order to free myself from a sense of limitation, this phrase empowers me to see that I am more than my responsibilities. A third phrase that I love to say everyday is, "Such truth that is the highest truth of who you are and the truth will set you free." It is easy to limit ourselves to the absolutes of life and see everything through a black and white lens of what is true and what is not true. In actuality, the truth I am referring to here is truth is the Highest truth, which is the only real truth that exists. What I mean by this is that there is an infinite number of individually-held perceptions of truth that are learned and subconsciously acted on by us as individuals. As these versions of truth become a collective perception of truth, they may become commonly accepted perceptions that allow even more individuals to believe this truth. However, this results in a truth that relies on the collective consciousness of those around us and not on the ultimate Higher Truth that is untouched by the physical world. This can really bring us down in many cases because we begin to define ourselves by what society labels as the truth. For example, the collective truth might appear to be that we are not successful unless we have a stable source of income and build a family of our own. This misconception can make those who struggle financially or are not interested in building their own families feel like they are failing in life. The Higher Truth, on the other hand, is an experience within yourself that requires choosing to strengthen your awareness of who and what YOU truly are. This Higher Truth requires that you listen to your inner power and not to what society deems as the truth. It is a matter of making a conscious decision to know and see the Power provided to you to be, do, and have whatever you choose for yourself.

Using our inspirations and readings to develop a collection of words of affirmation is very important to keep our minds growing and thus, strengthening our body-spirit connection. However, it is also equally important that you spend time building your own words of affirmation that you have a personal connection with. This can seem very intimidating, so I always suggest that you do what we should do when we feel this way. Take a step back, sit somewhere quiet where you can hear your thoughts, and reflect accordingly. I highly recommend meditation, but you can also achieve this by sitting alone somewhere you feel you can be yourself, using an app, or anything that works best for you. Once you have become one with your mind, it is time to ask yourself, What is the highest truth I can tell myself throughout the day that will help my current situation? For example, if you want a raise then your answer might be to tell yourself everyday, I am the most valued employee in my department. By telling yourself this, and really putting your heart into believing it, you feel that these words of affirmation will manifest through confidence, charisma, and how you carry yourself at work. With consistency, you will start to see wonderful results as you become more noticed at work and get that raise that you set out to achieve. It is more than just speaking something into existence. It is more about developing your mindset in a way that causes the attraction of these results and preparing yourself so that you are able to handle these big changes in your life.

Now that you have developed your list of words of affirmation, it is time to apply them to your daily life. There are many different ways that you can really implement these phrases and plant them deep into your mind. The first way is to look at your reflection in the mirror as you speak these affirmations and watch your body language when you are speaking. At first, this might feel a little strange, but with practice it should come naturally. Having the mirror in front of you ensures that you are speaking with strong body language. Your shoulders should be straight, your chest should be out, and you should look straight into your eyes when you speak. This body language will be carried into all your conversations that day if you wake up in the morning and practice. However, Words of Affirmation shouldn't just be limited to speaking. Another way to do this is by writing them down over and over. There is a proven connection between writing and memory so doing this will make sure that you are reminded of the affirmations on a subconscious level throughout the day. Another way is to have them visually in front of you by putting them where you will always see them. The best way to do this is to have different affirmations placed where you feel the most drained during the day. For example, place an affirmation regarding your wealth inside your wallet so that you can feel financially empowered even when making payments. Another example is to place an affirmation near the trashcan so you are not feeling guilty and beating yourself up when you have to throw away leftovers or spoiled food.

Perhaps placing your favorite affirmation on the car dashboard so that you look at it every time you drive to work in the morning. Ultimately, surrounding all your senses with the words of affirmation will allow you to retrain your mind to recenter itself whenever you are at risk of feeling even the slightest bit disconnected from your inner power. Consistency creates a compounding effect that raises the collective consciousness and thus helps you help the world.

CHAPTER 5

BODY CARE

∾

One of the major reasons why I always encourage being around nature as much as possible is because there is a strong correlation between Mother Earth and our body, mind, and spirit parts. If you think about Mother Earth, she has a core that is passionate and fiery within her very center. This intense core is responsible for the magnetic field that the entire sustainability of life on our planet depends on for survival. Her core, much like our spirit, is the foundation where all Her other layers emerge from and require in order to remain stable. Around Her core is the mantle that is located just underneath the Earth's crust. The mantle holds together the crust and depending on what happens at the core, shifts the tectonic plates of the visible earth above. The mantle, like our mind, is responsible for the evolution of Mother Earth's external parts that are visible to the outside world. Finally, Her crust is where we find the depths of the ocean, heights of the mountains, and stories of all living beings. Symbolic of our body, the crust requires the core and mantle to exist and its health is a reflection of what is going on underneath the surface.

With this in mind, we can imagine just how powerful the connection between our mind, spirit, and body is. What happens within will be shown above. Our body is our external part that allows our contained spirit to contact the material world outside. Through our five senses, we are able to relay what we experience back to our core. Understanding this connection allows us to better understand how our body communicates with us. It would make more sense now to comprehend why we might feel physical symptoms when we are experiencing internal unrest. We already looked at the connection between the spirit and mind and how this unrest could manifest itself through feelings of anxiety, depression, anger, or fear. However, to be able to truly know yourself, you must be able to notice what these symptoms appear as on the crust, on the outside. If the earth below the crust was poisoned, the life above it would cease to flourish. We would find draughts and wilting plants on the surface. Similarly, when our spirit and mind are not at peace, we might experience headaches, stomach pains, body aches, inability to stay still, and so on and so forth. The first step would be to understand your body language, as each one of us has a different way that our body speaks to us. The next step would be to learn how to treat these symptoms effectively by targeting the core issue of the problem, which is what is going on on the inside. The final step would be to establish a regular routine that helps keep you in that physically healthy state and keeps you feeling like the empowered individual that you are.

Taking a look back at our analogy of Mother Earth, we can see why it is easy to mistake the way we treat our physical symptoms. Of course, if our body is suffering from disease-related illnesses, then medication would be the way we treat the problem. However, working as a registered nurse, and being raised by one too, taught me that very often we can misunderstand what our body is trying to tell us. When our spirit and mind are not at ease, not only will we experience physical symptoms of mental distress, but we are also more likely to fall ill. The mistake we might find ourselves making is taking temporary measures to try and heal our physical symptoms. Very often, we have patients coming in and complaining about chronic headaches and yet after multiple tests, we find that the issue is simply that they are not taking care of themselves on a mental and physical level. These very same patients report taking painkillers on a daily basis to solve the issue without considering how they could prevent further headaches by targeting the root of the issue. I see this approach similar to one watering the crust of the earth that is going through a drought. Sure, it might help hydrate the earth temporarily but as much as you water it every day, the drought will remain because the earth itself lacks the ability to retain the moisture. With that being said, these patients are advised to take it easy with work to reduce the stress they experience on a daily basis, to make time for themselves to relax their minds, and to take care of their body.

Equally as important as understanding the connection between our body, mind, and spirit is learning the powerful skill of taking care of your physical health. The body is a sacred vessel for the soul and is meant to remain pure and filled with light. Without taking care of your body, the spirit and mind strength will find it difficult to manifest into your life as they will lack the essential connection to the outside world. You will find it difficult to complete the cycle necessary to tap into your inner power. Similarly to our previous practices of building our spirit and mind, the body self-care process also requires patience and time. It is a challenge to identify and unlearn habits from the past that might hold us back from growing. Incorporating the body into the emotional and spiritual healing process will not only transform the way we appear to the outside world, but it will allow us to work with the forces of Divine Intelligence and spiritual healing that is more accessible on Earth. By doing so, we will be able to let go of things that we have held onto for too long and felt difficult to let go of. You will find your entire physical being feels much lighter and easy-going by doing so. So now that we have learned how to identify the ways in which our mind and spirit speak to us through our bodies and the importance of really getting to know yourself so you can transform that language into action, now is the time to take that next step of practicing the art of self-care.

What I find beautiful about the body is you can almost feel the difference immediately after you begin to make changes to your lifestyle. Unlike spirituality and emotion that may be more difficult to directly associate with physical sensations, the body responds immediately to how we treat it. When we exercise, our endorphins release, giving us that feeling of peace and satisfaction. When we put on face masks, we can feel the dopamine levels rise at the sensation of our skin finally breathing. When practicing yoga or meditation to unite our inside being with our outside existence, we feel a peaceful and positive sense of calm with every subtle move. These physical sensations allow us to realize that the better we treat our bodies, the better we feel. Our moods improve, we feel more focused, we are more compassionate, we are able to act with a deeper love, and ultimately, we are able to enjoy life more. Yet on the other hand, when we mistreat our body or deny it what it needs and deserves, we feel the suffering. Our mind slows down, we feel the negative emotions stronger than usual, and fatigue clouds our ability to be ourselves and to be able to give others positivity. Just like we can't pour water from an empty cup, we are not able to serve from an exhausted vessel. Although I always insist on putting yourself first, it is also important to note that if you do not take care of yourself, you will also be negatively affecting those around you.

If reading this doesn't completely inspire you to find the motivation within yourself to take care of your body, I want you to think about everything your body does for you. It is the vessel that carries us through our life experiences from laughter with your friends, to sickness, to difficult and challenging times. It is our body that communicates with our children, lovers, and strangers. Our body gives others reassuring hugs and literally holds us together too. To care for this temple is not only a necessity, but it is a privilege. We only get one body in this life, and so we must treat it like so. Taking care of your body means choosing a healthy diet, exercising frequently, drinking enough water, caring for your hair and skin, using high-quality products that you research in advance, and even making sure to brush your teeth twice a day. From the little things to the big things, every attempt to care for yourself goes a long way. Often, I hear mothers complain that they do not have the time to care for themselves. This is understandable because they really are the superhumans who are responsible for the way we power through our childhood and adolescence. However, instead of being consumed with what they are not doing, I always ask them to focus on the little things they do such as brushing their hair, showering, eating breakfast, drinking a cup of tea before bed, and so on. From there, the motivation can be found to add on more little acts of self-love until you have reached a point where it is embedded into your daily life. Doing so allows us to constantly remind our bodies that we acknowledge that it is sacred and is deserving of all the love.

Taking care of yourself starts with what you put into your body and how you move your body. There are countless research studies that show that making good food choices reflects in other places in our life such as focus on work, our mood, symptoms of premenstrual syndrome, and how we sleep. We should keep our place of sleep surrounded with quality items that help us achieve a serene place to rest. Picture yourself trying to start a fire but the wood is wet, or perhaps trying to start a car with water-tainted gasoline in your car's trunk. If we instead use dry wood and good fuel, the fire ignites and the car will run smoothly. Similarly, if you put good stuff into your body, you will get good results! Moving your body every day, in any way possible, is also just as important as choosing what we put in them. Building the motivation necessary to work out or do any form of exercise can be difficult at first. The reason why we feel good after working out, and even better after doing it for consecutive days, can be explained by the science of our bodies. When we physically exert ourselves, the famous endorphins are released. Endorphins act as a natural painkiller to help relieve both pain and stress. A lesser-known fact is that if done on a regular basis, exercise can also help with the balance of more chemical messengers in our body. Dopamine, Norepinephrine, and Serotonin are all released when we exercise on a regular basis. Dopamine is responsible for the feeling of pleasure. Norepinephrine mobilizes our brain for action, allowing us to feel more energetic and focused. Serotonin is especially released when we exercise on a regular basis and is the reason behind our sense of well-being, improved appetite, healthy sleep cycles, and mood boosts. Finally, exercise can help with balancing the release of adrenaline. Usually when we are stressed, our body releases excess adrenaline and we are put into fight-or-flight mode. To remain in this state is extremely unhealthy and so by exercising, you are helping your body learn how to balance adrenaline. As you can see, exercise helps your body in many different ways and is the reason why doctors and nutritionists always recommend it as a part of almost any treatment.

Getting started on moving your body, especially if you have not done it in a while, can be challenging. For this reason, I suggest that you start with any form of movement that works best for you. For some, this might be daily walks after dinner. For others, it might be tennis, golf, swimming, yoga, pilates, or even karate. Doing some sort of movement on a regular basis can help your body ease into more physically exerting exercises that can push you to new heights. Once you are comfortable with the idea of moving your body on a regular basis, you can channel that confidence into trying to do something outside the box and outside of your comfort zone. If you have always wanted to try kickboxing, go for it! Perhaps you want to challenge yourself to complete a marathon too. You are the only one limiting yourself, and with the help of health professionals and fitness or life coaches, you should be able to accomplish anything you put your mind to. The best way to maintain that motivation is to follow the journey of someone who

motivates you. We often hear the criticisms of social media and the way it negatively affects our self-esteem, but I believe that it is what you choose to expose yourself to. If you pick to follow people that inspire you to become a better person, be it a fitness guru or a stranger on a weight-loss journey, you can actually utilize social media for the betterment of yourself. I personally follow countless women on different fitness journeys in various types of sports just so I can maintain the motivation and excitement to keep trying
new things.

At the end of the day, self-empowerment is making the time for your body. In doing so, you are amplifying your life in all aspects. Keep yourself educated on the different ways that you can care for yourself beyond exercise, hydration, and nutrition. For example, many do not know of the diets to help detoxify your pineal gland. This is a big part of the process of opening your third eye, which is fundamental in aligning your chakras. In Hinduism, it is believed that the Anja chakra is located at the center of the forehead between the eyebrows. Although it is not a part of the physical body, it is considered to be a part of the Pranic system. One of the reasons we apply a vermillion bindi between our eyes as Hindus is because this sacred spot corresponds with the pineal gland. The pineal gland is located in our brain and plays an important role in regulating almost every function in our body — from reproduction to growth to blood pressure to sleep and immunity. Unlike the rest of our brain, the pineal gland is not separated from the rest of the body by the blood-brain barrier; therefore, it has one of the richest supplies of blood, making it susceptible to toxins that build up in the body over time. Signs that you need to detoxify your pineal gland include sleeping too much or too little, headaches, difficulty with sense of direction, changes in fertility, osteoporosis, and mood disorders. So to help detoxify the pineal gland, it is suggested that you avoid fluoride, clean up your diet, eat food high in chlorophyll, pick dark chocolate over regular chocolate, drink chaga tea, eat organic turmeric, take iodine and boric acid supplements, and reduce exposure to EMFs. Just like this might be something completely new to some, there is an endless sea of information on the different ways to take care of your body. It all comes down to embracing that self-empowerment enough to make the time in your life to love and care for your precious body.

CHAPTER 6

THE POWER OF ROUTINE

~

Some people find a sense of drive and motivation by building their day around a routine. For others, the idea of having a predictable routine makes them shudder. We each have what works best for us. However the key, much like with everything else in our lives, is finding a healthy balance between the two extremes. Planning your day down to the minute can make you feel dissatisfied with your progress, especially because things almost never go according to plan. You might find that you are beating yourself up for not doing every single thing that you planned to do. On the other hand, not planning your day at all makes accomplishing goals much more difficult. More critically, without a plan you are unable to ensure that you are getting a healthy balance of work, self-care, spirituality, and caring for your loved ones. You will find that although you may check off all the things on your to-do list, you might fall short on making sure you are exercising enough, drinking enough water, spending time with your family, eating at least three meals a day, doing something you enjoy to take the stress off your shoulders, and so on and so forth. By implementing some sort of a loose structured schedule, you are giving yourself a sense of control over your day and life. With the implementation of this powerful habit, which will no doubt take practice and time to get used to, you will find yourself improving significantly in terms of focus, organization, and productivity.

Before delving into how to go about structuring your day, let's break it down a little more to help you truly fall in love with the idea of being in control of your day. When you wake up, you might have an idea of what your day or week will look like. Yet, by the end of the day or week, you might feel a sense of disappointment or dissatisfaction. You might feel productive in one aspect of your life but feel like you are missing out on the other aspects. So, what is the problem here? Time management. We hear this term all the time in high school and college or even from our parents. As a result, we might have a negative relationship with the idea of managing our time. I view planning my week, month, or year as a form of therapy. I make it as much of a comfortable part of my day as I possibly can. I turn the lights down low, light a candle, sit alone, and plan what I got to plan. Really throw yourself into the planning process. Close your eyes and picture how you envision your day going. How do you feel when you accomplish specific goals that day? The two main points you should keep in mind when planning your routine is to focus on the things you are able to control, such as meal times and meetings, and following a routine that supports your health. This means that your day-to-day activities should include staying active and well-rested, eating healthy meals on a regular schedule, setting realistic goals, mental-health check-ins, social time, and self-care time. The basic idea of a routine is not to ruminate on things you can't control, but to prepare for the unexpected challenges that might come your way.

What works best for you might be different to what works best for others. I have found that what works best for me is keeping checkpoints to ensure I have eaten well, reconnected with my spirituality, checked in on my mental health, spoken my words of affirmation, done some exercise for my body, and spent some time with friends and family. I then keep a checklist of things to do related to work and responsibilities that are more flexible and less constrained to time. To make things as least intimidating as possible, especially on days when there is an overwhelmingly large list of things to do, I prioritize by starting with the most important tasks. If there are family obligations, such as if you are a mother, then it is important that you build a routine around the tasks you need to do as well. Perhaps that means waking up early to do your workouts, eating breakfast with your children, and connecting with your spirituality during your kids' playtime. For those struggling with mental health or are recovering from a traumatic experience, I always encourage you to do as many of your activities with friends or family. Keep your support system close and aware of your plans so they can check in on you. Start your day with some sort of mindfulness exercise such as meditation and sitting with your morning beverage alone with a journal while your brain waves are at the optimal level of oneness. Most importantly, give yourself consistent check-ins for your mental health and spirituality. As you can see, how you structure your day will heavily depend on what you are going through. However, what remains consistent is that you are making the time for yourself. This is one of the most powerful tools of self-empowerment and can guarantee that you will be prepared for anything life throws your way. By building this sense of routine and normalizing making time for yourself, you are less likely to give in to feeling disconnected.

It is understandable that you might feel bad about yourself when you aren't able to commit to your routine. Instead of feeling bad, we should flip it into being proud of ourselves for attempting to make a change in the first place. That is completely normal in the early stages. The key is to learn how to shut off the internal critic if things don't go according to plan. This comes from loving yourself unconditionally. When the love you have for yourself surpasses your achievements, you will have the patience to forgive yourself and keep trying. There are many relationships that you may have in your life — whether it is with your partner, parents, or friends — and these relationships are important, so you make sure to put the effort and time into maintaining them and nourishing them. Yet, have you ever considered the energy you are not putting into nourishing the relationship with yourself? The more you begin to identify with yourself, the less you will hear the negative internal chatter that makes you question your worth — whether you are doing well enough, why you are not happy, etc. Each time you drift away from your healthy habits, cut yourself some slack and recenter yourself. Write down a list for yourself that you can read to remind yourself of all the benefits of planning a routine so you can reignite the inspiration needed to get back on track.

I picture building a routine similar to the process of baking a cake. If the cake was a symbol of your success, then routine would be the stack of healthy habits that build up the cake. Habit stacking is the process by which you link together a chain of small actions into a routine, where the sum becomes more powerful than the little parts. This can throw off people because if they fail to see the bigger picture, they might question why it is taking so long even though they are taking lots of action to manifest success. It is all about understanding that a cake cannot be built by stacks of habit chunks. You have to break these habit chunks down into individual ingredients. It is also important to be patient while the cake pieces bake in the oven. Repetition of the baking process ensures that your cake becomes more stable over time. With practice, you will have memorized what ingredients in your cake of success works best for you. You will understand more about what happens to the consistency of the cake batter when you remove and add ingredients or small actions and how they will impact the stability of the stacks of health habits. With time, you will also come to understand that timing and patience are key in making sure that the cake bakes to perfection and that any impatience can set you back to step one of the cake-baking process. Most importantly, you will realize that the icing and decorations of the cake, or how the world outside sees your progress, is not nearly as important as what is happening on the inside of the cake. The decorating part will come, but only after you have mastered the art of baking and stacking effectively.

So now that we have addressed the importance of getting to know the recipe cake of success as well as the back of your hand?, I am not sure what this means, the question is what ingredients to start with. The first thing is to build your routine around a specific time or place. This will help anchor your routine to something that is unchanged. A couple of examples of this are what you do when you first wake up, the first and last things you do before and after work, things you do during your lunch break, or even your workout routine for each day. The second thing is to build your routine gradually, preferably working on a single routine for a month before you start adding anything to it. This will ensure that you do not overwork yourself trying to achieve everything at once, and also it keeps your willpower strong. Although we looked at the main three aspects of self-empowerment as being your body, mind, and spirit, your routine should consist of the seven following main areas: productivity, relationships, finances, organization, spirituality, physical and mental health, and leisure time. By having small wins every day in each of these areas, you can build the necessary momentum. The different ingredients that you decide to put into your recipe of routine to accomplish these small wins should work seamlessly together. For example, if you do not have the time to watch the documentary you've been wanting to watch for a long time, why not just watch it as you eat your lunch? Maybe do your skincare routine before you start working so that you can leave the mask on as you do your finances. Never look at routine as simply blocking out time for what you need to do and more like a recipe that requires all ingredients to work together. What keeps the cake standing straight and stable is accountability and motivation. Accountability makes sure that you are completing what needs to be done in the time you assigned it and helps build discipline. Motivation can come from giving yourself small rewards after completing tasks so that you aren't burning out. With time, you will add and remove ingredients of the cake to adjust to what you feel works best for you.

There are dozens of ways in which a routine can help you develop a sense of self-empowerment. For starters, a routine helps you feel more efficient. You will spend less time trying to decide what it is you want to do and more time channeling your internal confidence of knowing what it is you have in mind to get done. Taking too much time trying to decide how to move forward can make us second-guess ourselves and question our purpose. Having a list keeps us focused on the ultimate goals and less on wondering what should be our next step. A lesser known fact about routine is that it grants you the freedom to do what you wish. By wasting less time on things that are not propelling you to your ultimate purpose in life and doing more activities that solidify you goal, you are carving out more time to spend on yourself during your free time — all whilst feeling productive about your day so you are not overwhelmed by guilt when you take a day off. Routine allows you to break the bad habits, form healthy habits, and develop the essential skills necessary to accomplish your goals. Through repetition, we can replace all our bad habits with good habits that match our goals and aspirations and get even better at what we are working on with each day that passes. And if you do fall off track, create a way to make the activities fun, maybe refresh your sitting meditation area or purchase luxury loungewear to wear when you are doing self-love care. If you find that you barely make the time to meditate and get in touch with your spirituality, through routine and repetitions, you will find that after a month of practicing meditation, you will feel a big difference if you miss a single day. Just like building the habit of brushing your teeth before bed, consistency is the secret weapon to build these skills and routine.

Ultimately, it is through routine that we can keep track of our progress toward achieving our goal. I find that it is more empowering to define success by how far you have come rather than by the moment you accomplish the goals you have set out for yourself. Goals and aspirations, especially big ones that are going to make a significant impact on your life and on others, are rarely achieved overnight. There are many steps we must take and by planning it out, we can break down big steps into smaller, more achievable steps. A sprinter does not accomplish breaking her record simply by practicing every day. She must also make incremental adjustments to her training practices every day and week so that she is ensuring that she is making the progress necessary to accomplish her goal. Routine planning will allow you to identify where you are falling short, where you need to cut down on time spent on an activity, and where you need to adjust to hold yourself accountable for the vision you have within your heart. The benefits of having a routine are endless, and we could go through them all, but at the end of the day it will come down to your sense of satisfaction that you will feel once you navigate the world of routine and time-management skills. You owe this to yourself in order to bring your inner power out through self-love and by building the foundations of your body, mind, and spirit.

CHAPTER 7

SETTING BOUNDARIES

~

We always hear about the importance of setting boundaries for yourself as a means of self-empowerment, but what does this really mean? Boundaries are essential to healthy relationships and ultimately to a healthier life. Throughout this book, we have looked at all the different ways you can empower yourself from within. We can take a look back at the analogy of the towering oak tree that is now flourishing as a result of the Power it found within itself while growing its roots of spiritual intelligence, the sturdy trunk of emotional intelligence, and the branches of your rational intelligence as a result of repetitive healthy habits. Your branches are now filled with deep green leaves that are bursting with fruitful positive energy and delicately spotted leaves in which your acorns of wisdom lay, ready to be shared with the world. You are at your peak, your most powerful state of being. You are the epitome of empowerment. How do we keep ourselves in this state and protect ourselves from any external energies that could possibly bring our towering progress back down to its knees? Boundaries. When we start to activate through spirituality, we strip off the layer of emotions and we start to feel our feelings in the truest form. When I came to recognize my emotions as keys to a part of me that needed to be unlocked and released, it was not a familiar type of experience, but it is what was needed to see the truth of the story. Boundaries is yet another tool of success that makes sure that all your discipline that you put into yourself to get the results you got isn't going to default you off the route that you are driving on after a bad argument, a breakup, a death of a loved one, or even getting fired from your job. If any events that challenge you do arise, take the time to reevaluate everything and place yourself where you need to be and establish a more loving approach. There comes a time where we must look at the situation and adjust some relationships so we can hold space for ourselves and the other person involved; even the closest relationships need space to gain a different perspective so you can keep your power and not give it away.

You might be wondering what boundaries have to do with coping with traumatic experiences. Boundaries are what keeps you independent and separated from the influences of the outside world. Unfortunately, these boundaries you set for yourself are not as obvious as physical fences or signs that we see on the road. Rather, they are more like invisible bubbles that must be reinforced for others to know that they exist. This might be a difficult aspect of your life to navigate, especially if you are someone that is used to giving and helping others. It comes down to communicating these boundaries to ensure that you are protective of your health and well-being. In some cases, boundaries will also keep you safe from harm. Boundaries are the ultimate capstone of self-empowerment because they give you a sense of agency over your physical body, space, and feelings. There are various parts of your life and identity where setting boundaries are most important. These include your personal space, sexuality, emotions, thoughts, possessions, time, energy, and cultural or religious beliefs. You might find it easier to be protective and to communicate your boundaries in some areas than in others. For this reason, it is important to truly get to know yourself and where you feel you have people in your life that are overstepping these boundaries and making you feel uncomfortable or are limiting your growth. This self-reflection can be painful at times because it really makes you realize the underlying truth behind relationships. Not knowing your boundaries not only limits your growth, but it will put you on a path of unraveling all your progress.

Looking back at my own life, there was one profound experience that really taught me the importance of setting boundaries and differentiating between a healthy connection and an unhealthy, limiting attachment to someone. I met my first boyfriend at a very young age, around fourteen or so, and he was much older than me at the time. He was a young Puerto Rican fellow that swept me off my feet and really made me believe I had found true love. I met him one summer at his house when I went over with mutual friends. We started talking shortly after, which led to officially dating. Since my parents were set on me marrying an Indian man, they completely disapproved of this relationship with an American boy. By the time I was sixteen, I was convinced that I was truly in love with my boyfriend. I adored everything about him, from the way he made me laugh to the way being around him made me forget everything that I didn't want to deal with. When I was with him, I wasn't worrying about my parents' approval, or my grades, or how dissatisfied I felt with myself. I felt like he completed me, because at the time, I had not understood what it meant to be at peace with myself. I thought this love was real, but in reality, it was deep codependency that was built on a foundation of unhealthy attachment. Around this time, I was getting really fed up with my parents' grip on how I lived my life. I felt like I was drowning in the overwhelming pressure that they put on me as to what direction I should be headed in life. I had no sense of control over my life, decisions, and who I was. There was one night where I overheard my father telling my mother that if I were ever to get pregnant at my age, he would disown me. I know now that he was speaking out of a place of frustration and fear of losing me to the commitment, I had to end my toxic relationship. At the time I didn't understand that, so hearing this made me feel like the world was being sucked under my feet. The more I felt detached to my purpose and family the more I depended on my boyfriend as an outlet for these feelings.

So one day, I decided it was time to leave home. My parents had taken me out of school and transferred me twice just so I would be as far away from him as possible. So I got in touch with him again and we made a plan for me to run away from home. I remember that day so vividly, like it was just yesterday. I packed a few of my belongings, pulled on a scruffy pair of jeans and a black shirt, and hopped into my car. I drove my car to a nearby store and taped a letter for my parents. I told them why I was leaving, why I couldn't stay there not here? anymore, and that I was in love with this guy. So we went to New York to stay with his sister for two to three weeks. That was when I started to see a completely different side to him. He changed the way he treated and spoke to me. He became increasingly emotionally abusive. I felt like I couldn't stand up to that because it would mean that we ran away for nothing and that was too difficult of a reality to accept. From the start, I knew deep down that he wasn't the perfect guy. He went to an alternative school that had a reputation for where all the "bad guys" went to school, but I didn't understand that the red flags I was being given were a sign to step back and set the boundaries necessary to find myself. Since we didn't have a lot of cash on us, we decided to find a job. His sister tried to help us but since it was my first time being independent, I couldn't land a single job. This entire experience gave me the opportunity to gain some level of street-smart intelligence, which was probably one of the few positive sides. At this point, we had grown exasperated. We were running out of money, and his sister couldn't keep us with her forever.

Despite the conditions and his mistreatment of me, I still was not ready to go back to the life I had with my parents. As difficult as it is for me to say this today, being in that situation gave me the biggest sense of control over my life that I had ever had. So we decided to move to North Carolina to get married. At this point, his sister began to worry so she called my parents. Getting on the call with my parents was probably the most challenging part of the entire experience. Hearing my mother crying and hearing the pain in my father's voice as they pleaded for me to come home made me realize that the way I was coping with the stress of their overprotective love was not the right way at all. Instead of communicating my feelings and the need for boundaries to them, I had turned around and ran away from the problem. So I agreed to come home and they booked me a plane ticket for the very next day. I had expected to come home to anger and punishment but instead my dad took me out for breakfast.

"Have I ever told you the story of the monkey?" he asked, as he looked at me deep in the eyes.

"The monkey?" I replied, puzzled.

"Yes. The monkey. See, there was a monkey that was put in a container with her baby. She held on to this baby because she loved it so dearly. Slowly, the container started to fill up with water and the monkey knew that she had to do something to save her little baby. Do you

know what
she did?"

"No. Jump out?"

"No, she couldn't jump out of the container. They were trapped. So she did what she could do best. She held up the baby as high as she could so the water would not touch her. She held her baby so high that even as the water reached above her head and she was fully submerged, the baby could still breathe. This is the love your mother and I have for you."

It was then that I realized the depth of the love my parents had for me. Their overprotective suffocation was coming from a place of unconditional love. They were doing what they thought was best for me. I felt so misunderstood, but the biggest lesson I took away from this experience was that the only way I should have dealt with this situation was by communicating myself to my parents instead of running away from the problem. By doing so, I had done more damage than had existed before. It took a while for me to build my relationship with my mother again. She was extremely hurt and didn't understand what she did to deserve what I had done. Not only did I feel like I needed to regain her love and reconnect with her but I also had to do the same with myself. In the process of learning the importance of boundaries, I began to take the first step in the right direction of self-empowerment. When I went back to school, my dad dropped me off at the front doors. I saw my ex standing by his car outside, waiting for me so we could talk things out. I looked right past him and walked through the front door and that was the last I ever saw of him. I feel like that moment was truly symbolic of the control I gained over my life. I had made the mistake of thinking that giving into the relationship that I depended on for a sense of freedom was how I could gain control of my life, but I was wrong.

At the end of the day, I am so grateful that this experience took place. It was very painful and I hurt others in the process, but it taught me the lessons I needed to learn. I learned more about myself than I had ever done at the time. I felt so much stronger when I came out the other side. My sense of independence did not come just from being far from home. It came from making the decision for myself to come back home. I found that I was capable of getting through things on my own and from that moment onward, I decided that I wanted to be independent no matter what. That independence, however, must come from the powerful skill of setting boundaries. Women need to achieve success on their own and not feel like they have to be in a relationship in order to feel successful. Many of us make the mistake of feeling empty because we are single and lack a partner in life. We mistake this incomplete relationship with ourselves as loneliness because we need someone else to fill in the gaps. It is our duty to take our power back as women and do things on our own just because we can, even though society tells us otherwise.

Just like there are chemical messengers released from our brain when we exercise, there are also chemical messengers that are released when we do things that give us pleasure. These messengers, such as dopamine, can become addictive. Sometimes, we can find ourselves getting addicted to the wrong things and that can be toxic relationships. Being able to identify these violent cycles of neurotransmitter release in the body when in toxic relationships can really help you know when it is time to step out and set your boundaries. Boundaries do more than just protect you as a physical being, they can keep your spirit safe too. Keeping yourself protected from negative energies will ensure that you keep your inner spirit light and pure. When we have our boundaries overstepped and we do not know how to communicate ourselves, this feeling can manifest itself as hateful and hurtful language and action. Just like with all other phases of growth, learning to set your boundaries requires that you sit alone and reflect. Think of your past and present and tune into your feelings. Ask yourself what makes you feel most comfortable and able to be yourself? What makes you feel suffocated and unable to be who you truly are? Name your limits and write them down. Make sure that you are constantly practicing self-awareness so that you are able to bring out your inner feelings about relationships and their impact on your well-being. Be assertive in what you deserve, and seek help where you need the support. By starting small, you will be able to use the valuable tool of setting boundaries to make your self-care the priority. When you are on an airplane and they tell you what to do in the case of an emergency, they always say that you should put your oxygen mask on before you help others. Without your own oxygen mask, you are unable to help others and make the impact you dream of making. Be direct and unapologetic with what you want to say to others because the only person you should ever feel like you should be asking for permission on how to live your life is you. Get that power back.

CHAPTER 8

FINANCIAL EMPOWERMENT

~

Most of us worry about our finances. After all, we need money to keep a roof over our head, eat healthy food, treat ourselves, and provide for our loved ones. On the spectrum of those who worry about money, some completely avoid dealing with their financial problems while others think too much about it. Either way, both are signs of an unhealthy relationship with your finances. Becoming financially empowered comes from a deeper rooted confidence in yourself and your success. It means unlearning the fear of success and facing these fears with bravery and honesty. It requires that you sit down, reflect, and be real with yourself. This feeling of insecurity and doubt you have of your financial situation will always be reflected in the way you carry yourself and even how you do business. In order to become a financially empowered woman, you must build a positive relationship with money. In doing so, you will overcome any avoidance anxiety that you have when dealing with money and create a loving environment around the idea of money.

Often, our fear of success might be a result of something that happened in the past or in our childhood. For some, it might be a failed business endeavor, losing money unexpectedly, or even getting fired from a job that provided you financial security. These experiences can affect you on a deeper level and define the way you view your own financial success. They might make you question your potential, shy away from the attention that comes with financial success, and ultimately limit your overall sense of self-empowerment. We can even fear money. Fear is a liar and it can cloak itself as being protective or even comforting. You can say the words, "I receive and spend money with ease" out loud. Let yourself really stretch and start to be curious. What would you do if you made exactly the amount you truly wanted? The devil can hide in corners and make it appear that you are just fine where you are. It's time to get yourself out of the autopilot that may not be serving you as well as you thought it was. God wants you to cash in on your abundance and dive into the truth of who you really are. And there is no time like the present. For me, it was my experience as the only kid on the honor roll. The sense of isolation that I felt by being the only one who achieved grades so high made me step back and fear being successful. Without realizing, I internalized this reservation well into adulthood. Once I gained my power back, I came to the realization that we as women should feel like we are doing what we love without worrying about money. This doesn't mean to avoid dealing with it, but rather approach building a stable income as a means to become free.

To build a healthy relationship with money requires effort and commitment to identify what you think about yourself. This relationship is deeper than financial security. It is a loving and supportive measure for yourself. Be honest and ask the right questions. Am I balancing my checkbook correctly? Am I making the time to plan out my yearly budget? Did I set financial goals that are in alignment? What did I do to establish a steady flow of income? Am I taking care of my finances so my finances can take care of me? Make this reflection with yourself as enjoyable as possible. Light a candle and drink your favorite cup of tea as you map out your financial plans, even if it takes a couple of days a week to complete. Sometimes, talking to God as you plan your finances will help you feel even more empowered. The more you discipline yourself with money in a loving way, the stronger this relationship will become. Make your time with your finances fun — light a candle, get some luxuries supplies, and create a loving atmosphere. Building a healthy relationship with your finances also means pushing yourself to overcome bad habits. Open that bill you've been avoiding and deal with it. Over time, your relationship with money will begin to unfold and you will find that you've allowed for abundance to come to you easier.

Financial empowerment also means showing up for success even if it isn't what you thought it was going to be, or what you were raised thinking it would be. Your parents' idea of your success might be completely different from what you envision your success to be. This is not something that you should run away from, but rather embrace as a means of understanding who you are as an independent woman. Reach out of the box and set goals that are so big that in the moment, they don't feel real. Write those goals down and then break it down into steps and start taking small action toward that goal. Watch how your confidence in your success manifests into confidence in your finances. More important than gaining this confidence is maintaining it. Going back to the words of affirmation, how you speak to yourself will affect this confidence too. Make sure to include words of affirmation that strengthen your bond with your financial self. Remind yourself gently that you are not a victim of your financial situation. Tell yourself everyday: "I love money and money loves me." Financial confidence also comes from surrounding yourself with the right people. I found that the best way to overcome my fear of success that I embodied from my childhood was to put myself around other women who inspire me to be financially successful. If you admire someone, get around people who are like that person. Connect with them, grow your relationship with them, and mirror their life approaches. From learning more about yourself and your money story to redefining your idea of success, you will be able to become the completely financially empowered woman that you have always been.

CHAPTER 9

TRUSTING THE PROCESS

~

Through every aspect of the journey, from strengthening your spirituality to growing your mindset to building a routine, the emphasis on being patient with yourself has been consistent. One of the biggest reasons why people tend to fall back into old habits is because of the lack of apparent progress. It can sound a lot easier when we compare this to going to the gym, for example. We often hear that you need at least a month of consistency to see any real progress. But what happens when you go for two months and you still don't feel like there was any progress? It all comes down to your definition of "progress." It is easy to come up with obvious indicators of progress such as an increase in education, health status, or income. However, to define progress by these indicators is detrimental to our feeling of success. We tend to picture progress as moving in an upward direction when in fact, growth is almost never linear. Rather, growth that appears to be linear and only in one direction can actually be destructive over time. It is important to understand that as we grow our capabilities and resources, this does not eliminate threats. This growth might solve previous challenges but will bring about more challenges to deal with. For this reason, viewing growth too simply can make you feel like no matter how hard you are trying, things just don't get easier. In reality, the healthiest way to view progress is to understand the dynamic relationship between capacity and challenge.

Picture yourself on an adventure through an unknown forest. At the start of the walk, you are unaware of how to navigate the unknown intertwining paths ahead of you or even what is hidden in the shadows. So, you take the first bold step, clutching onto your backpack of resources. In this backpack, you have a map, a compass, and a book on how to start a fire. You read the book before you decided to embark on this journey and you tried to practice starting a fire on your own but you have yet to start one on an actual adventure. As you take the first few steps, you feel your heart race and palms sweat with a mix of anticipation and fear. You trudge ahead anyways, eager to reach the other side of the forest, a place of peace that you've heard so much about. At first, the unknown feels overwhelming, so you decide to stay on the path with as much light as possible so you don't have to risk getting lost. However, you start to realize that this easier path might feel more comforting to navigate, but there's just not enough opportunity to find food and safety for the night. The trees are bare and the sound of animal's echoes in the air. So, you grab your backpack and begin to unpack the resources that you have collected to prepare you for the journey. It takes some time before you plan the path ahead of you using just a compass and a map, but you eventually decide on the direction you should take. You pick out a few options ahead of time, in case something goes wrong.

The thought of taking the more fruitful but less-traveled path makes you feel nervous again. So, you sit down and reflect on how far you've come, how comfortable you feel compared to when you first started the journey, and how capable you were to take actions and learn in order to move yourself in the direction toward opportunities. You internalize the reality that it is time to take the next step out of your comfort zone in order to reduce the potential threats of being out in the light and grow your capacity to handle the darker path by relying on your fire-starting skills. So, you grab a handful of twigs, tie them together, and light the tips on fire to help navigate the dark. As you get deeper into the forest, you begin to find all the undiscovered fruits hanging from the trees waiting to be picked. The air is so still with silence that you can hear yourself breathing. You pick off some fruit and climb a tree to sleep for the night. You are on the path less traveled and are finally comfortable with the idea of stepping outside of your comfort zone. You smile to yourself as you fall asleep, grateful for the growth you've made to adapt to becoming the person you have to be to reach the goal you set out to achieve. You carry on this path for a couple more days, weeks, months maybe. By the time you see the end of the forest, you're a completely different person than you were at the start. Some days, the journey was difficult, other days it was much easier. You climb out of the dark and into the light. Ahead of you is an endless array of pristine blue crater lakes with flocks of birds flying in and out of the surrounding trees and a community of laughing people sharing stories and playing cheerful music. You made it. You savor the moment and take a deep breath. You close your eyes and think to yourself, where is the next adventure going to take me?

As you reach each milestone, you will find that you are even more excited for the next one. Empowerment doesn't mean reaching your goals and settling. Empowerment is found in the process of reaching your goals and in the preparation of embarking on the next journey that follows. If you aren't feeling like you're making any progress, sit with yourself and have a practice to recenter yourself. Reflect and ask yourself the questions. Is there an outside influence that is telling you that you can't have what you're aspiring for? Is it an internal dialogue stemming from your childhood? Sometimes, the biggest reason we feel like we aren't making progress is because we are comparing our chapter two to someone else's chapter eight. Focusing on your own lane is more than an over spoken cliché. If you were focused on how far others were on the path through the forest, then you would lose focus on your own efforts and how far you've come. The only time you should look at what others are doing is when you are searching for positive inspiration.

Sometimes, the changes within yourself might not be clear until you are put in a situation that you handle differently than you would have in the past. One of the most profound moments in my adulthood where I came to this realization was after being sexually assaulted at thirty-two. When I was a hospice nurse, I met a woman through a mutual friend. We decided to meet for dinner and immediately hit it off. I trusted her and so when she asked me whether I wanted to go out later that night with her and her friends, I agreed. The night went well at first. We met up with her fiancé and his friend. However, as the night went on, I began to lose focus and realized something was wrong. Someone had put something in my drink and sexually assaulted me. When morning came, I was feeling like a mess. I no longer felt safe, especially because I was new to the city. I had put my trust in the woman had no idea what her fiance and friend had done. Although I was deeply affected by this traumatic experience, I choose not to feeel like a victim. The next day, one of the men called me up to ask me to go for dinner, and I knew at this point that he was just trying to confuse me and make sure that I didn't go to the police. I was lucky that at the time I was receiving some counseling on my Hospice Nursing duties, and while it did help, I only wish I had support on how to deal with my traumatic experience as a nurse. However, what stood out to me was the way in which I handled the experience and didn't blame myself nor define myself as a victim from this experience after years after the event and daily meditation. Instead, I was shown another way to release both myself and them with compassion. I chose to see it from a higher perspective and focused on seeing my mission through it all. Tapping into my inner power allowed me to forgive them and understand that these people were coming from a place of conditioning and they were just lost. You won't just feel the growth when faced with traumatic experiences. The growth can be reflected in the most subtle ways, such as the way you handle a disagreement with your partner or your coworkers.

Another issue that might be the reason why you are not feeling progress is because you are not taking accountability for your actions. Taking on a goal, especially the bigger more ambitious ones, comes with a big responsibility. You're going to be the person who looks back and sees the mountains that you chose to climb or not to climb. It is all up to you. There is no one that is going to be checking on you for every step you take, asking you why you did or didn't do something. Every action you take has to come from a place of intention. The reason that you decided to go after a goal is going to fall on you. Your actions have to be contributing to building a healthy stack of habits that will propel you away from threats of success and toward opportunities and abundance. Accountability is usually a problem when you fail to place an emphasis on self-awareness, reflection, and being real with yourself. If you do not get to know yourself on a deeper level every single day and build the confidence necessary to give yourself honest unbounded self-evaluation when you need it, then you will continue to lack accountability. Accountability is more than just "calling yourself out," it is about taking action to change the way you are doing things. You can either choose to continue on the path of blame and shame, or you can build the skills necessary to act upon reflection. Without accountability, you will continue to doubt yourself and question whether you are capable of your goals. Ask yourself the questions: Where do I want to be? What kind of life do I want to have? What kind of friends do I want to attract? What impact do I want to have? You might find that there are coverings that you might not even be aware of, and you need to peel away those coverings by holding yourself accountable whether or not it feels uncomfortable to do so. Your comfort zone is a lie. It is a place where we just sit and decide to be okay with what is going on in our lives, but deep inside we know it is not what we want. I am not saying you have to be uncomfortable; I am saying don't let your success or your vision be too small. Let your highest vision of yourself be your comfort zone. Never settle.

CHAPTER 10

IT IS YOUR TIME

~

Your time is now. There is a reason you decided to pick up this book and take the first step to self-empowerment and uncovering your inner power. Perhaps, you feel like you are stuck and can't seem to find what you need to do to propel your life in the direction you want it to go. Empowerment comes from taking that first step in building the life you want to have and living your life the way you want to live it. To do this, you must be willing to let go of what isn't meant to be and allow yourself to attract what is. Not only should you prioritize learning more about what tools to use to take yourself on this journey of uncovering your inner power, but you must also be willing to ask for help when you need it. Finding the right coach can help you redefine what your mission is and can have a powerful impact on the process. Your heart is your number one fan and has always been, so it deserves tender care and attention. It all starts with acknowledging that it is your time, and it has always been your time.

A lot of women tend to feel guilty for setting boundaries and putting themselves first. I did it myself where I reached a point in my life where I felt the pressure of having to take care of my elders and those around me. I soon realized that I have to take care of myself first before I could manifest that strength and clarity into helping others. Women, especially those with a lot of traditional expectations of what a woman should be, lose sight of that in their lives. You might find it difficult to say anything other than yes, even when you don't want to. Helping yourself is respecting yourself enough to know that your health and happiness is the most important and valuable gift that you could give yourself and the world around you. Life can be a roller coaster and if you don't cut that time out, you can find that years have passed where you didn't care enough for your well-being and that could spark internal feelings of self-resentment. It is important above all else because in doing so, you are releasing yourself from the guilt and self-resentment that has piled up over the years. Setting boundaries to focus on your growth could mean that you don't call certain people or make time for them because you need that time for yourself. Even if that means cutting out two weeks, a month, or even a year to focus on yourself. Now is the time to say no to what doesn't serve your purpose and let people know when you need to take time off for yourself. This is the most difficult part because it can hurt to feel like what you are doing is wrong or selfish. The key is to stay focused on the fact that by helping yourself, you are able to give yourself and others around you much more, whether it is your family or your customers in business.

There was a time where I felt the most disempowered as a woman, but I didn't know where I was falling short. I was living on my own, paycheck to paycheck, and had no sense of control over my spendings or the direction of my life. What was blinding me was that I wasn't being honest with myself. I didn't understand how to unblock what was standing in the way of attracting abundance. Taking this first step is a responsibility that you owe to yourself and your future, no matter where you are in your life right now. The material world will always be there, but you need to first build the foundation for yourself. I used to want to treat myself to things that I simply couldn't afford and when I found that no matter what I spent money on I was still unhappy, I knew that I was going about things the wrong way. It can be easy to find yourself comparing yourself to your friends if they have houses or luxury bags but once you internalize that these things will always be there, you can focus on getting yourself in a situation where you can get whatever you want whenever you want it. Have a dream in your heart and work toward that dream. Keep on visualizing this dream and borrow from your future life experience to make your dream your reality. Speaking your desires into existence can come from the little things, even if it is just walking into the mall and looking at all the things you want to buy and just tell yourself, "that's mine, I already have it" instead of "I wish I could afford that." In doing so, you will begin to feel the confidence in yourself which will manifest in all aspects of your life.

The unexpected is always inevitable, so you should feel solid within your own thoughts. Cut out your life into where you ultimately want to be on a weekly, monthly, and yearly basis. Practice meditation and look at your life around you. Tap into your inner power through prayers and regular journaling. Start by setting small goals such as waking up earlier than everyone else in your household. Make an area in the house that is just for you, your own personal space. Women tend to play many roles in their life and stretch themselves out thin. When you begin to make these changes to your life, you don't even have to tell everyone everything that you are doing because outside influences can really affect the process.

This journey takes a big commitment to yourself, and you don't need what others tell you. You need what is found within you. Silence your life for a bit so you can synchronize with that goal within. Write out your priorities and keep it simple at first. For example, your priority might be to have the house in top order by the end of the week, or to get your meditation practice to be ten minutes a day, or perhaps you decide to run twice a week for the next month. These priorities that you set for yourself will get you to a place of momentum and keeping that commitment to yourself will give you the confidence to take the next steps to empowering yourself. The next time you decide to do something to change your life, reflect on why you want to make this change. Why do you want to take that second job? Is it because you need the extra money, or is it because that is where your passion lies? Find a coach who can help you get into the direction you want and invest into tools to help dig deeper into your desires and what you really want out of life. Have a clear perspective of what you want and cut everything else in your life out.

The journey to uncovering your inner power might be overwhelming at first, but setting incremental steps toward your final goal and trusting the process will make the journey to reaching the top of the mountain one-jedi-butt-kicking kind of a story to tell.

Bibliography

1. https://languages.oup.com/google-dictionary-en/
2. *Spiritual Intelligence : The Ultimate Intelligence*; Danah Zohar

www.ingramcontent.com/pod-product-compliance
Lightning Source LLC
Chambersburg PA
CBHW070127100426
42744CB00009B/1758